BEETHOVEN

For my husband Ezra,
whose loving support inspired this book.

First edition for the United States, Canada,
and the Philippines published 1994
by Barron's Educational Series, Inc.

Design: David West Children's Book Design

© Copyright by Aladdin Books Ltd 1994
Copyright in the text © Ann Rachlin / Fun with Music

Designed and produced by
Aladdin Books Ltd
28 Percy Street
London W1P 9FF

All inquiries should be addressed to:
Barron's Educational Series, Inc.
250 Wireless Boulevard
Hauppauge, NY 11788

International Standard Book No. 0-8120-1996-2

Library of Congress Catalog Card No. 94-10114

Library of Congress Cataloging-in Publication Data
Rachlin, Ann.
Beethoven / Ann Rachlin; illustrated by Susan Hellard. – 1st ed. for the
U.S., Canada, and the Philippines.
p. cm. – (Famous children)
ISBN 0-8120-1996-2
1. Beethoven, Ludwig van, 1770-1827–Childhood and youth–Juvenile literature.
2. Composers–Austria–Biography–Juvenile literature. [Beethoven,
Ludwig van, 1770-1827–Childhood and youth. 2. Composers.] I. Hellard,
Susan, ill. II. Title. III. Series: Rachlin, Ann. Famous children.
ML3930.B4R33 1994
780'.92–dc20   94-10114
[B]   CIP AC MN
Printed in Belgium
13 12 11 10 9 8 7 6 5 4 3

Famous Children

BEETHOVEN

ANN RACHLIN
ILLUSTRATED BY SUSAN HELLARD

BARRON'S

Ludwig went to school with his brothers. He hated his lessons. He studied French, Italian, and Latin but his marks were very poor. As for mathematics, poor Ludwig was so bad at multiplication that if he had to find the answer to three times four, he would write down four three times and add them all together!

Kaspar and Nikola were very good at school. But when it came to music, no one was as brilliant as Ludwig!

Ludwig was so small when he began to play the clavier that he had to stand on a bench to reach the keys. He also learned the violin. His father, Johann, was a singer. He gave Ludwig his first lessons, but was very strict.

Coming home late at night, Johann would drag Ludwig out of bed to practice. If Ludwig tried to play from memory, his father would become very angry!

"What silly rubbish are you scratching now?" he would scream. "Scratch from the notes – otherwise you will never be a real musician!"

Sometimes when his father was busy with visitors, Ludwig would creep up to the clavier and play some chords.

Then Johann would lose his temper.

"What are you messing around here for? Go away or I'll box your ears!"

But even his bad-tempered father had to admit that Ludwig was making excellent progress. Soon the little boy was learning how to play the viola and the organ. Already he was a much better musician than his father!

When Ludwig was seven years old, his father decided that his son should give his first concert. He had heard how, some years earlier, Leopold Mozart had taken his brilliant little boy, Wolfgang, on a concert tour. "Ludwig shall earn money, too!" he said.

The concert took place on March 26, 1778. All the notices said that Ludwig was only six years old. Johann lied about his son's age so that people would believe Ludwig was as clever as Wolfgang Mozart.

Johann was making a hole in an egg! Ludwig made a face as he watched his father suck out the raw egg and then eat two prunes!

"He's going to sing tonight," thought Ludwig. His father always ate a raw egg and prunes before he sang.

"It keeps my voice fresh!" he told his young son.

As Ludwig grew up, he realized that almost everyone he knew worked for the Archbishop of Cologne. Life at the Archbishop's palace was very grand, as the Archbishop was an important person. He was one of the few "Electors" who chose a new Emperor when the old one died. He loved good food, hunting, and music.

The Elector had his own orchestra. Ludwig's grandfather had been the Elector's kapellmeister – master of the chapel – the leader of the court musicians. It was Johann's dream that one day Ludwig might become a kapellmeister too.

When Ludwig was ten years old, Christian Gottlob Neefe became the Elector's new organist. This fine musician realized that Ludwig was a genius who needed a gentle, understanding teacher who would encourage him to compose. Mr. Neefe soon declared that young Ludwig was "a young genius of most promising talent. He will certainly become another Wolfgang Mozart if he continues as he has begun!" Mr. Neefe appointed Ludwig as his assistant organist.

Early one morning, Ludwig was awakened by a cock crowing on the roof above his parents' room. He woke his brother Kaspar.

"There's a cock on the roof, Kaspar. He looks very plump! Let's catch him!"

The two boys crept downstairs and into the baker's kitchen where they found a piece of bread.

Standing in the yard, they tempted the cock with the bread.

"Here, cock-a-doodle! Down here, come down!"

The cock could not resist and flew down to snatch at the bread.

"Got you!" the two boys cried.

At dinner that night, their parents had no idea who had caught the tasty bird they enjoyed so much.

"Time for you to go upstairs, Mama!" The boys were very excited. It was their mother's birthday and name day and every year they celebrated with a concert. While Mama was resting, a special chair was placed under a canopy and decorated with leaves and flowers. By ten o'clock everyone was ready and the musicians began to tune their instruments.

"She's coming! Everyone be quiet!"

Mama came down the stairs. She looked beautiful. Johann led her to the special chair. The musicians began to play, and the sound of the lovely music resounded throughout the neighborhood. After the concert, they ate and drank. Then they all kicked off their shoes and danced in their stocking feet, so they would not disturb any neighbors who were sleeping.

Ludwig was sitting at the window of his bedroom, overlooking the courtyard. In front of him lay the manuscripts of his first important compositions. They were three sonatas for the clavier. He had worked on them for weeks, rewriting long passages until at last he was satisfied. He wrote the dedication,

"To the Right Worthy Archbishop Elector of Cologne, my gracious Sovereign, composed by Ludwig van Beethoven, age eleven years."

"Bring me a list of all the musicians in my orchestra!"

In 1784 a new Elector arrived in Bonn. The Archduke Maximilian was the Emperor's brother. He was a very fat man who loved good food and good music.

"What's this? Johann van Beethoven has a very stale voice! You say his son Ludwig is still young, but very capable. Plays the organ, does he? I shall look forward to hearing young Ludwig play!"

Ludwig was not scruffy anymore! Now that he was a court musician, he had to look very neat and tidy. He wore a smart frock coat, knee breeches, silk stockings, shoes with bow knots, and an embroidered waistcoat with pocket flaps, bound with real gold cord. His hair was curled at the side with a pigtail at the back. He even had a sword, on a silver belt, that he would sometimes wear on special occasions.

When Ludwig was 16, Mr. Neefe decided that he should study with Mozart in Vienna. After a long journey, Beethoven arrived on April 7, 1787. A few days later, he met Mozart, who invited him to play. Ludwig sat down at the clavier and played brilliantly. But Mozart did not seem very impressed.

"Good, you prepared that well," he said in a rather cool manner.

"I can do much better than that!" cried Ludwig. "Give me a melody and I will show you what I can do with it!"

Ludwig's fingers flew across the keyboard. He was playing for the great Wolfgang Mozart. He was inspired. The simple melody that Mozart had given him became a masterpiece as Beethoven wove it into a wonderful composition. Mozart sat enthralled. Finally he went over to some friends who were sitting in the next room.

"That is Ludwig van Beethoven!" he said. "Someday he will give the world something to talk about."

Ludwig van Beethoven became one of the world's most important composers. He wrote over 600 works, including nine symphonies, five piano concertos, one violin concerto, one opera, 32 piano sonatas, and many string quartets, trios, and choral works. Beethoven composed many of these masterpieces after he became deaf. Among his most famous pieces are "The Moonlight Sonata," The "Pastoral" Symphony (No. 6), and "The Ode to Joy" from his Symphony No. 9. He died in 1827.